BANBURY
THEN & NOW

IN COLOUR

MALCOLM GRAHAM & LAURENCE WATERS

First published in 2011

The History Press
The Mill, Brimscombe Port
Stroud, Gloucestershire, GL5 2QG
www.thehistorypress.co.uk

British Library Cataloguing in Publication Data.
A catalogue record for this book is available from the British Library.

ISBN 978 0 7524 6342 1

Typesetting and origination by The History Press
Printed in India
Manufacturing managed by Jellyfish Print Solutions Ltd

CONTENTS

ACKNOWLEDGEMENTS

Unless otherwise stated, the old photographs are from the extensive collections of Oxfordshire History Centre, Oxfordshire County Council. Other images are reproduced by kind permission of the *Banbury Guardian* (pages 16–17 and 22–23) and the *Oxford Mail & Oxford Times* (pages 18–19, 20–21, 24–25, 26–27, 52–53, 54–55, 60–61, 68–69, 80–81, 88–89, 90–91).

ABOUT THE AUTHORS

Malcolm Graham was Oxford city's first full-time local history librarian between 1970 and 1974 and then local studies librarian for Oxfordshire County Council until 1990. He was then appointed head of Oxfordshire Studies, managing a busy major resource for local and family history until he retired in 2008. A keen local historian, Malcolm has published extensively on local history and given hundreds of talks and broadcasts over the years. He was awarded a PhD by Leicester University in 1985 for a study of the development of Oxford's Victorian suburbs and is a Fellow of the Society of Antiquaries of London.

A retired professional photographer and photography teacher, Laurence Waters has written or contributed as co-author to twenty-seven books on local history subjects. His main interest is the Great Western Railway. Laurence is the honorary photographic archivist for the Great Western Trust at Didcot Railway Centre.

INTRODUCTION

In 1901 the population of Banbury was 10,012, and Marjory Lester recalled the town in her childhood as being like something out of a fairy story with its old shops and houses, and livestock sales in the streets. Banbury developed as the market centre for the fertile farming area known for centuries as Banburyshire, and its traditional trades and industries grew almost entirely out of the products of agriculture and stock rearing. Cheese, cakes and ale were major products in 1610 and the last two remained important until recent times. The arrival of the Oxford Canal in 1778 boosted local industries, and a boat-building yard, later Tooley's boat yard, opened in 1790. The making of agricultural implements initially served the local market but the industry took on a new dimension when Bernhard Samuelson acquired James Gardner's business in 1849 and transformed it into the Britannia Works. The railways, reaching Banbury in 1850, contributed to the success of the Britannia Works and smaller firms by providing swift access to more distant markets.

The Agricultural Depression caused Banbury to stagnate after 1871 and many people left the area or emigrated in search of employment. The transformation of Banbury began when Midland Marts Ltd transferred livestock sales to a new cattle market in Grimsbury between 1925 and 1931, leaving only the weekly provision market in the streets. The Northern Aluminium Co. Ltd, later Alcan, opened its factory in Southam Road in 1931, and the company's workforce reached 2,300 during the Second World War. Other key firms were attracted to a new industrial estate created in Southam Road in the 1950s. Banbury welcomed 'overspill' families from London and Birmingham and proposals to expand the population to 70,000 were narrowly defeated in 1966. Growth has continued more slowly but about 45,000 people now live in the town. The opening of the M40 in 1991 placed Banbury at the heart of the motorway network, encouraging further industrial development, and job opportunities attracted around 6,000 Poles to the town by 2006. In 1998, the sudden closure of Banbury Cattle Market, described as the largest in Europe, ended centuries of tradition but the Castle Quay shopping centre, opened in 2002, now draws customers from well beyond Banburyshire.

This book features two excursions around the town centre, the first from Banbury Cross to Castle Quay and the Market Place and the second (from page 50) taking in High Street, South Bar and George Street. Laurence Waters' photographs, taken in March and April 2011, contrast with older views and show how change has affected Banbury's 'fairy story' streets. Supermarkets and branches of national firms have largely replaced small, locally-owned businesses but many older buildings survive above modern shopfronts and historic façades have sometimes been retained. Away from the main streets, slum clearance, traffic management and commercial development have left few old buildings in once-populous districts. Pedestrianisation has greatly improved conditions in the town centre since 1991 and the Oxford Canal, once virtually hidden from view, is now a major attraction.

BANBURY CROSS

BANBURY CROSS AND some determined onlookers in the early 1900s (left). The cross was designed by John Gibbs of Oxford and was built in 1859–60 to mark the marriage of Queen Victoria's eldest daughter, the Princess Royal, and Prince Frederick William of Prussia. It was thought to be, but is not, on the site of one of Banbury's medieval crosses, which were destroyed by Puritans in the early seventeenth century. Gaslights were placed around the cross in 1888. To the right, the offices of the Banbury Board of Guardians were built in 1900–1.

THE REMOVAL OF Banbury Cross as a traffic hazard was discussed in 1927, but the 'roundabout system' was introduced in 1930 and is still in use. Statues of Queen Victoria, Edward VII and George V were added to the cross in 1914 and the railings were removed in 1927, making it easier for revellers to climb the structure. Banbury Museum took over the former Banbury Board of Guardians' offices between 1981 and 2002 and a day nursery now occupies the building.

SHEEP SALES

FARMERS AND DEALERS gather round the sheep pens in Horse Fair in the late 1870s (left). Sheep sales were held in High Street until 1656 and the top end of High Street down to the White Lion was known as Sheep Street until the nineteenth century. Traders moved reluctantly to Horse Fair but the area outside the George and Dragon became the established place for weekly sheep sales. The premises of the printer J.A. Taplin are visible away to the right at No. 29, next to the Woolpack pub.

SHEEP SALES AND their attendant smells were cleared out of Horse Fair in 1931, and a public convenience in local stone was built in 1981 outside the former George and Dragon pub. Car parking takes up some of the space but pedestrians have a tastefully paved area complete with seats from which they can watch the world go by.

HORSE FAIR

BANBURY CROSS AND Horse Fair in August 1933 (left). A car keeps left around the cross and a woman ambles casually over to the structure. The statue of Queen Victoria, installed in 1914, looks down upon the scene and road signs point the way for eagle-eyed motorists. The single-storey County Garages are visible on the left.

BANBURY CROSS, RESTORED in 1979, is now the centrepiece of a more formal roundabout but it has been a quieter spot since the opening of the M40 in January 1991. Along Horse Fair, the Whateley Hall Hotel incorporates parts of the former Three Tuns inn and this block also houses the Odeon cinema, which opened as the Regal in October 1940. Away to the right, restoration work masks the familiar outline of St Mary's church tower.

NORTH BAR

A QUIET AFTERNOON in North Bar in about 1930 (right). Advertisement hoardings cover the façade of Percy Gilkes' newsagent's shop at No. 32 Parson's Street, where a dog stands guard by a parked bicycle. In the early 1920s Stranks' restaurant was a popular stopping point for men driving new cars from the Midlands to London showrooms; by this time it had blossomed into a hotel but still offered breakfasts, lunches and teas and catered for coach parties. Beyond Stranks', a gateway provided rear access to the Buck and Bell at No. 39 Parson's Street.

BANBURY CONVENIENCE STORES now occupies No. 32 Parson's Street where paint has obliterated the Victorian brickwork; blocked windows are still a reminder of the old adverts. A new Buck and Bell was built on the site of Stranks' in 1935 after the old pub in Parson's Street was converted into two shops.

SOUTHAM ROAD

SOUTHAM ROAD FROM North Bar in 1939 (right). The mid nineteenth-century Three Horseshoes pub obscures the entrance to Castle Street and the Three Pigeons beyond it. More nineteenth-century houses are followed by the gables of St Mary's Church of England School, rebuilt in 1900 on the site of Banbury National School (1817). Children from Banbury Workhouse attended St Mary's school, being marched every day down Warwick Road by a burly ex-regimental sergeant major 'with a big voice, and useful walking cane'.

DEMOLITION OF THE Three Horseshoes exposed the Three Pigeons pub to view, and Merisham Court is a recent addition beside St Mary's school. The Three Pigeons is an attractive ironstone building with a thatched roof and dates from the seventeenth century; in the early 1800s it was used for meetings of the Hundreds of Banbury Manorial Court. Its semi-subterranean appearance is the result of the realignment of North Bar in about 1826.

WARWICK ROAD

BANBURY GENERAL MOTOR Garage in Warwick Road in the early 1920s (left). The garage was established in part of the old Austin's brewery behind North Bar in about 1920 and prospered in this key position near the junction of the Warwick and Southam roads.

PEOPLE'S PLACE, A substantial development of apartments in mid-Victorian Banbury style, now occupies the corner of North Bar and Warwick Road. The garage closed in the early 1970s and the site, including surviving parts of Austin's brewery, was cleared in 1993 in readiness for a new courthouse, which was never built.

COMPTON STREET

COMPTON STREET LOOKING south from Castle Street East in May 1969 (left). This cul-de-sac of twenty houses was built in the 1870s and 1880s. Cicely Bailey recalled the properties as 'very nice, small and clean, the roadway being stoney, as the council never "made it up" '.

BANBURY CASTLE WAS slighted after the Civil War, and the north side of the Castle shopping centre, occupying the site of Compton Street, provides a 1970s interpretation of the castle complete with a 'dry moat' and 'battlements'. A footpath to the right of the building takes the pedestrian swiftly from this roundabout at the end of Cherwell Avenue to the very different townscape of Cornhill and Banbury Market Place.

FACTORY STREET

FACTORY STREET LOOKING east from Castle Street North in April 1969 (below). Factory Street took its name from Cobb's horse girth factory between the Oxford Canal and the river Cherwell. It extended from a covered passage beside the Plough on Cornhill to a drawbridge over the canal and was home to Mold's, Banbury's only tripe and cow heel shop.

THE CASTLE SHOPPING centre obliterated Factory Street in the 1970s but this shopping mall (above) is on the same alignment. Built at a cost of £4 million, the development provided twenty-eight shop units behind the Market Place and included the International Supermarket and premises for Boots and W.H. Smith. It was officially opened by the Duke of Gloucester on 3 May 1978 and is now part of the Castle Quay shopping centre.

TOOLEY'S BOATYARD

TOOLEY'S BOATYARD ON the Oxford Canal in the 1970s (below). The boatyard was opened in 1790, just twelve years after the canal opened to Banbury, and narrow boats were built there until commercial traffic declined in the 1930s, from which time, the yard specialised in

repair and refurbishment.
At the point where the canal
narrows, a wooden drawbridge
carried Factory Street across
the water until the late 1960s.

TOOLEY'S BOATYARD
CONTINUES to flourish
in a scene that was totally
transformed by the building
of the Castle Quay shopping
centre between 1998 and
2002. The glazed bridge links
the new Banbury Museum
away to the left (which opened
in 2002) with the tourist
information centre and the
shopping mall. Further away,
the lifting bridge above Banbury
Lock has been reinstated.

OXFORD CANAL

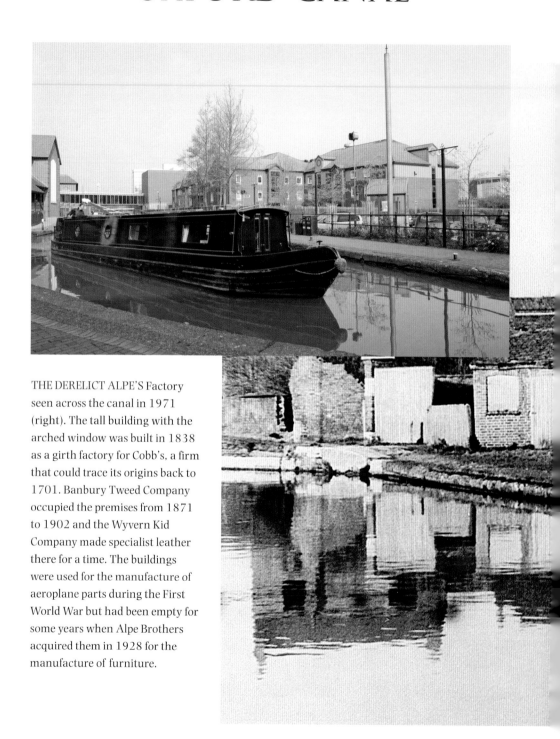

THE DERELICT ALPE'S Factory seen across the canal in 1971 (right). The tall building with the arched window was built in 1838 as a girth factory for Cobb's, a firm that could trace its origins back to 1701. Banbury Tweed Company occupied the premises from 1871 to 1902 and the Wyvern Kid Company made specialist leather there for a time. The buildings were used for the manufacture of aeroplane parts during the First World War but had been empty for some years when Alpe Brothers acquired them in 1928 for the manufacture of furniture.

CHAMBERLAINE COURT AND, beside the glazed bridge, Banbury Museum now occupy this historic industrial site (left). The narrow boat approaching Banbury Lock symbolises the increased recreational use of the canal, which is now very much at the heart of everyday life in the town and the focus since 2004 of an annual Banbury Canal Day.

BANBURY MILL

BANBURY MILL IN 1970 (right). The buildings date from the eighteenth century, but the mill is perhaps on the same site as the Bishop of Lincoln's mill recorded 500 years earlier. Between 1878 and 1961, the mill was operated by the firm Edmunds & Kench, and on his way to and from the 'Rec', Arthur Jones saw sacks of corn being hoisted up into the building and horses being watered in the nearby stream. He also recalled the flock of Rhode Island Red hens that climbed a plank to their roost in the stores every evening.

ONE OF BANBURY borough council's last decisions was to establish a Spiceball Park Leisure Centre based in and around the old Banbury mill. The Mill Arts Centre opened in 1974 and other facilities were added in 1977. Recreational use of the nearby mill meadow goes back to 1867 when a private

company established a park and swimming bath, which the borough council took over in 1889. The unusual name 'Spiceball' is said to derive from the spicy faggots made by a Bridge Street butcher, Mr Waddoups.

CORPORATION WHARF

OXFORD CANAL AND the old Banbury
Corporation Store in January 1975 (right).
This wharf, approached from Mill Lane, was
established in 1825 by the newly formed
Banbury Paving and Lighting Commissioners
to receive stone and other materials. Banbury
Corporation inherited the wharf in 1889 and
continued to use it until local government
reorganisation in 1974.

A CAR TRANSPORTER on Bluebird Bridge,
which carries Concord Way across the
Oxford Canal. The Corporation Wharf was
lost to Banbury's inner relief road in 1990–1
and Concord Way now continues Cherwell
Street northward, carrying traffic to and
from Hennef Way. The bridge is named after

the former Blue Bird Commercial Temperance Hotel, which flourished in Bridge Street between the wars. Trees beyond the bridge announce the nearby Bridge Street Park.

THE TOWN HALL

MARKET DAY IN Bridge Street or Cow Fair in the early 1920s (right). A lively scene outside the town hall when cattle were still being penned along both sides of the street; local lads could hope to earn 6d by 'cow bunting', that is by looking after cattle at the market and then driving them to their new owner's field. A motorist is trying an adventurous route through the crowd and a local bus awaits passengers beside the lamp post.

CATTLE SALES BY auction were transferred to the new Grimsbury premises of Midland Marts Ltd in 1925 and private sales followed in 1931, leaving Bridge Street a cleaner and, for a time, quieter thoroughfare. The growth of traffic gradually filled the vacuum, and the area outside the town hall became a very basic bus station until the late 1960s. Bridge Street is now much more pedestrian friendly and all but a few local bus services go from the nearby bus station in Mill Lane.

BRIDGE STREET

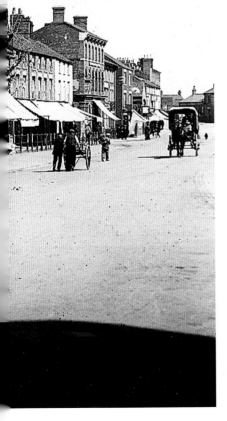

THE NORTH SIDE of Bridge Street on a peaceful afternoon in the 1920s (left). H.O. White's corn, seed and coal merchant's business occupied No. 43, the gabled building on the corner, with Atkins & Co.'s oil cake business to the left on the corner of Mill Lane; the entrance to Banbury Wharf is just visible on the other side of Mill Lane. Down Bridge Street, the tall building with a prominent cornice was the Cadbury Memorial Hall, built in 1876 as a Temperance hall, and its facilities included hot and cold baths. With adjoining buildings, it later became the Waverley Temperance Hotel and then the Blue Bird Commercial and Temperance Hotel. Part of the building was used as a labour exchange for men between the wars.

PLANE TREES WERE retained when the Castle Quay shopping centre took over this part of Bridge Street between 1998 and 2002. A Debenhams store fills most of the view but the varied treatment of the frontage gives the impression of several different buildings. Further down, the façade of the Cadbury Memorial Hall was retained and today's bar and restaurant keeps alive local memories of the old Blue Bird Hotel and the building's founder, James Cadbury, a local Quaker and uncle of George Cadbury, founder of the Bournville factory.

33

THE OLD GAOL

THE OLD GAOL in Market Place in about 1910 (right). Erected as a wool market by Banbury Corporation in 1610, this building probably became the town gaol in 1646. The Blue Coat School, founded in 1701, used the upper floor until the early nineteenth century. In 1852, the inspector of prisons described the gaol as the worst that he had ever seen, and the gaol was closed in 1854.

THE CORE OF the building has survived but the portion now occupied by O'Neill's hairdressing salon has been unsympathetically re-fronted and two of the three gabled dormers have been lost. Easily missed plaques on the upper floor of both parts of the building recall its surprising history. To the left, the former Fox pub has been converted into a shop.

MARKET PLACE

A DOG TAKES the air in a quiet Market Place in the early 1920s (left). Two youngsters try out bicycles from Curry's shop at No. 7 on the far left; further along, at Nos 9–10, a huge dustpan on the wall advertises Nathan's hardware shop, which has stock spilling out into the roadway. The Palace cinema advertises a double bill and Robins' ironmonger's shop is prominent on the corner of Butcher's Row.

EXCEPT ON MARKET days, cars have taken over Market Place, but the view is remarkably unchanged. Taylor's the estate agents are now at Nos 7–8, the four-storey building on the left, and Nathan's premises are occupied by A-Plan Insurance. A Cargo Home Shop occupies Robins' distinctive two-gabled timber-framed building.

THE UNICORN

MARKET DAY OUTSIDE the Unicorn in the mid 1860s. Many Banbury buildings were destroyed during the Civil War when the Royalist-held castle was besieged in 1644 and 1646. The Unicorn, probably built in 1648, was an early and striking replacement and the building was certainly an inn

by 1676. John Cheney, landlord of the Unicorn, began printing here in 1767 and Thomas Hunt, the founder of Hunt, Edmunds Brewery, started brewing on the premises in 1807. Beyond the Unicorn, Charles Pettit's drapery shop occupied the so-called Prebendal House, a building of the 1660s re-fronted in the eighteenth or early nineteenth century.

THE BRICK-PAVED AREA outside the Unicorn, which was restored from a poor condition by the Nationwide Building Society between 1971 and 1973, can be seen above. In the 1930s, Kays Modern Food Stores had taken over the shop in front of the Unicorn and emblazoned their slogan 'Kays Ways Pays' across the gabled dormers. Next door, the Prebendal House was given a very plain ironstone frontage during a drastic restoration in the early 1970s.

MARKET PLACE FROM THE UNICORN

THE MARKET PLACE from the Unicorn in about 1878 (below). Carriers came to Banbury on market days from every significant place within ten miles and nearly 300 were said to attend the market in 1854. Some of their carts are visible here and there are produce stalls outside some of the shops. Most of the activity seems to be concentrated near the Angel on the corner of Castle Street where pigs were generally sold.

MARKET DAY IN Banbury when stalls still occupy a little changed Market Place (above). Historic façades on the left were carefully preserved in the 1970s when the Castle shopping centre was built and, out in Bridge Street, mature plane trees mask the changes brought by the Castle Quay shopping centre.

CORNHILL

CORNHILL IN ABOUT 1920 with a railway parcels van outside B.R. Morland's stationery shop (right). Gillett's Bank, established in 1822 and rebuilt in 1847, is behind the ornamental lamp post and bank manager, William Charles Braithwaite (d. 1922), lived at Castle House, down to the left. The Plough pub in the bank's shadow had an off-licence window visited in the evenings by old ladies seeking medicinal gin or whisky. Next to the Plough, the impressive Vine was built as a corn exchange in 1857 and converted into 'a very large "barn" of a pub' in the 1880s. The goddess Ceres on the roof of the building had lost her head during a storm in December 1900!

GILLETT'S BANK WAS taken over by Barclays in 1919, and the Cornhill branch closed down in the 1930s, becoming the local headquarters of the St John's Ambulance Brigade for many years. The eighteenth-century Castle House survives as offices in the shadow of Banbury's multi-storey car park. The Plough has gone but the frontages of the Vine and other adjoining buildings were retained during the Castle shopping centre development in the 1970s. A new statue of Ceres was installed above the old corn exchange façade in 1983.

THE ORIGINAL CAKE SHOP

CHILDREN GATHER OUTSIDE The Original Cake Shop in Parson's Street during celebrations for the coronation of Edward VII in 1902 (right). Banbury cakes were first mentioned in 1586 and their fame spread in the eighteenth century when Betty White and her husband Jarvis owned The Original Cake Shop. The shop was taken over by Mrs. E.W. Brown in 1872 and the date 1638, marking the beginning of cake making on the site, was added to the façade during a subsequent restoration of the premises.

THE PLAZA BALTI restaurant and Fashion Fabrics now occupy the site of The Original Cake Shop. The last Banbury cakes were baked at the shop in May 1967 and a property company submitted plans for a shopping development to include The Original Cake Shop and properties up to Church Lane. Local campaigners battled to save the building but demolition started in April 1968; a building preservation order came too late to save one of Banbury's most historic structures.

PARSON'S STREET

PARSON'S STREET IN the 1920s looking east past the Reindeer Inn (left). The bust of William Shakespeare was formerly a pub sign for the Shakespeare Tavern, which flourished between about 1869 and 1903; the building later became a registry for domestic servants. On the right, beyond John L. Pilsworth's prominent millinery and ladies' outfitter's shop, stepladders on the pavement suggest that painters were at work on The Original Cake Shop.

A HANGING SIGN for the Olde Reine Deer Inn still adorns Parson's Street, which is now brick-paved and almost traffic free. The bust of William Shakespeare now sits above a very different Photofinish shopfront at No. 46. Down towards Market Place, Parson's Street has retained much of its character but development in the late 1960s claimed properties on the right beyond Church Lane.

THE REINDEER INN

THE GLOBE ROOM in the yard of the Reindeer inn in about 1900 (below). The Reindeer inn is first recorded by that name in 1664 but the building dates back to the mid sixteenth century, with substantial additions in 1570 and 1624. The Globe Room was an extension of the highest quality

built in 1637, incorporating excellent oak panelling and a fine plaster ceiling, and it was clearly intended to attract the most prosperous travellers. The inn later declined because it was badly placed for coaching traffic.

THE GLOBE ROOM remains but the old service building of about 1600 beyond it has been removed. The Hook Norton Brewery Co. sold the Globe Room panelling, the ceiling and other fittings for £1,000 in 1912 and these items were thought to have been exported to the United States. In 1964, however, the panelling was traced to a furniture factory in Islington and it was brought back to Banbury, being restored to the Globe Room in 1981. The plaster ceiling had been stored elsewhere in London and was perhaps destroyed by bombing during the war.

COW FAIR

BANBURY TOWN HALL from Cow Fair in about 1880 (right). The town hall, designed by the Oxford architect Edward Bruton and built in 1854, dominates a market day scene of cattle and parked carriers' carts. The building was partly funded by the town's MP Henry Tancred and by Lord Saye and Sele. A dinner and a soiree for 600 people were held to mark its completion in October 1854 but it was another six years before the clock was installed. The Corporation's fire escape ladder can be seen against the town hall wall next to the men's urinal. Lamprey's seed merchant's shop is visible away to the right at No. 34 Bridge Street.

PLANE TREES WERE planted in Bridge Street in the 1890s and they have flourished in the urban environment. They provide welcome shade in summer but have obscured much of the townscape. The town hall is now only glimpsed from this spot but preserved advertisements are just visible on Lamprey's old shop, which closed in 1980 and is now occupied by Champion Recruitment. To the right, the brick frontage of Banbury's Marks & Spencer store is visible through the trees.

PAST THE TOWN HALL

HIGH STREET FROM the town hall in 1956 (right). The traffic seems light but parked cars occupy all the available space at the roadside. Beyond the town hall, commercial premises included Leach's sweet shop and the half-timbered building occupied for many years by the Refuge Assurance Co. Ltd.

BRICK PAVING, VICTORIAN-STYLE street furniture and an extraordinary Tardis-like public toilet are elements of the High Street pedestrianisation completed in 1991. The plane tree has flourished and, past the town hall, the ashlar stone façade of the NatWest Bank is a prominent feature.

THE BAPTIST CHURCH

THE OLD AND the new in Bridge Street in June 1967 (left). Special offers attract a throng of shoppers and their cars to a brash new Fine Fare supermarket on the site of the Catherine Wheel pub. To the right, the Baptist church had also been built on the site of an old inn, the Altarstone, in 1841. The fine Ionic portico originally had three pairs of columns and two entrance doors, but the columns were rearranged in 1903 to provide a central entrance.

FINE FARE EXPANDED into the former Baptist church in about 1972 but the portico was retained, looking uncomfortably like a film set creation. The premises are now separate again with Bonmarché in the original supermarket building and Family Bargains behind the portico. Shrub and tree planting has helped to restrict car parking and a flower stall occupies space outside Barclays Bank, a dignified 1930s building fronted in local stone.

VIVERS' HOUSE

THE EAST END of High Street in the late 1930s (left). The view is dominated by Edward Vivers' splendid timber-framed and gabled house, which was built in 1650. For many years, the building was occupied by Brown's Banbury Cakes and by the ironmonger's, Neale and Perkins. The parked vehicles include a van from Colebrook's the fishmongery at No. 6, but Neale's were still defying the traffic by displaying goods in the roadway. They are remembered as selling 'everything you could imagine in the way of tools, household wares, nuts, bolts, screws and oil lamps'.

VIVERS' HOUSE STILL graces a High Street that was pedestrianised in 1991 and its current occupants include Mr Simms Olde Sweet Shoppe, Timpsons and Jenny's Café and Restaurant. Thomas Cook occupies the red brick building next door, which was for many years Timothy White's and Taylor's chemist's shop. The 1970s NatWest Bank is the only major change in the longer view towards the town hall.

HIGH STREET

HIGH STREET, LOOKING west past the Red Lion in the 1920s (below). The Red Lion dated back to the late fifteenth or early sixteenth century and Marjory Lester recalled that it was always bright

with tubs and hanging baskets. It was at the hub of Banbury life, a venue for auction sales, Corporation dinners and trade in corn and seeds on market days. On the right, Boots the Chemist advertised prominently at Nos 79–80 and is remembered for a large flashing sign on the roof that was visible all over town.

WOOLWORTH'S ACQUIRED AND demolished the Red Lion for their 3d and 6d store, which opened in 1931; the firm closed its Banbury shop in the 1980s and the premises are now occupied by Mothercare and Santander. The former Boots store is now more discreetly occupied by the jeweller Michael Jones; further up, the three-gabled property on the corner of Church Lane was replaced in about 1930 by a typical Burton's store.

HIGH STREET FROM BUTCHER'S ROW

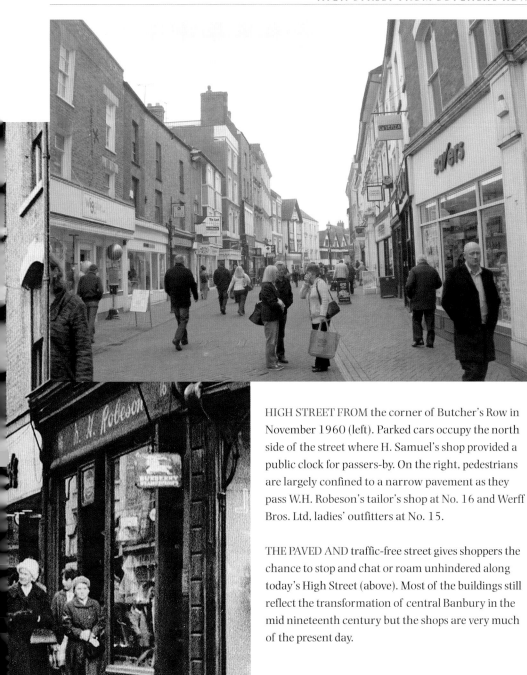

HIGH STREET FROM the corner of Butcher's Row in November 1960 (left). Parked cars occupy the north side of the street where H. Samuel's shop provided a public clock for passers-by. On the right, pedestrians are largely confined to a narrow pavement as they pass W.H. Robeson's tailor's shop at No. 16 and Werff Bros. Ltd, ladies' outfitters at No. 15.

THE PAVED AND traffic-free street gives shoppers the chance to stop and chat or roam unhindered along today's High Street (above). Most of the buildings still reflect the transformation of central Banbury in the mid nineteenth century but the shops are very much of the present day.

THE WHITE LION

A CYCLIST WHEELS smartly round a distracted pedestrian outside the White Lion Hotel in the 1950s (below). The White Lion was first recorded in 1554 and Marjory Lester recalled it as the best hotel in town, beautifully furnished with antiques and equipped with windsor chairs and pewter

tankards in the bar. Managed by Jim Thewlis between 1948 and 1972, the White Lion was noted for its cuisine but its trade subsequently declined and the hotel closed in 1975.

THE BUILDING WAS restored in 1978 to form an attractive entrance to the White Lion Shopping Walk. The White Lion reopened as a pub in 1995 and marks the beginning of the High Street pedestrian zone, which was instituted in 1991. In the background, Burton's store closed in the late 1970s and the building, now occupied by Moss, has lost its original Burton up-stand.

TOWARDS BANBURY CROSS

CHILDREN AND CYCLISTS enjoy the freedom of the High Street in the 1900s (below). Blinds on the right protect shop displays from the afternoon sun and a lamp hangs outside the White Horse. On the corner of Calthorpe Street, H.C. Fisher ran a Bible Society depot at No. 32 High Street for a few years from about 1905.

HIGH STREET TODAY has widened pavements, road markings and necessary segregation between pedestrians and vehicles. The view towards Banbury Cross is dominated by the clock bracketed out from Anker's premises on the corner of Calthorpe Street. This was erected in 1911 by F.W. Ginger, a clockmaker, jeweller and optician, to mark the coronation of George V. On the right, beyond the zebra crossing, Banbury's former post office is now the Exchange pub.

CALTHORPE STREET

THE LIVELY COMMUNITY of Calthorpe Street celebrates VE (Victory in Europe) Day in May 1945 (below). Calthorpe Street boasted three pubs, the Plough, the Globe and the Black Swan, and a huge range of trades from banana ripener to whitesmith; Cheney's printing works was located there from 1896 and W.G. Cheney is standing in the centre of the group in the photograph below wearing a white linen jacket.

PICTURESQUE BUT NEGLECTED, Calthorpe Street has almost entirely gone and its community with it. Cheney's gave way to the Marlborough Road car park and a short-lived Sainsbury's supermarket, now the Calthorpe Centre, in 1986. Higham's Solid Fuels building is the last remnant of Calthorpe Gardens, a vanished cul-de-sac built in the 1870s. Further on, the removal of Hyde's furniture factory revealed the tower of St John's Roman Catholic church, built in 1838.

SOUTH BAR

SOUTH BAR NEAR the junction of Bloxham Road in 1968 (right). The town's South Bar or gate stood here from the thirteenth century until 1785 when William Judd, a local carrier, obtained permission to demolish it as an obstruction to traffic; Judd's commemorative monument was removed in 1843 because it had become a magnet for layabouts. The Classical style terraced houses opposite were built in about 1835 and, to their left, the Case is Altered pub, formerly the Weavers' Arms, dated back to the seventeenth century.

THE CASE IS Altered and Nos 28–34 South Bar were demolished in 1973 and Alcan House, offices for Alcan Aluminium UK, occupied the site in 1978. The block now has other occupiers and has been renamed

South Bar House. In the foreground, the surviving K6 telephone box has been joined by a street tree, a bus shelter and a pay station for the nearby car park.

SOUTH BAR
LOOKING DOWN

A SMALL DOG controls the approach to South Bar in about 1910 (below). South Bar became magnificently formal in the 1820s and 1830s as the Banbury Paving and Lighting Commissioners

realigned the road and created a regular footpath on the west side. They also planted trees in an attempt to beautify the street in 1826, but vandals made short work of them; the lime trees visible now were planted in 1885.

LIKE ST GILES' in Oxford, tree-lined South Bar has proved attractive for car parking. Despite the removal of much through traffic by the opening of the M40 in 1991, the Bloxham Road junction is still very busy and no place for idle loitering, whether by dogs or humans. On the left, South Bar House replaced Nos 28–34 in 1978.

OXFORD ROAD

OXFORD ROAD LOOKING down towards South Bar in about 1930 (right). The embanked pavement graphically illustrates how much the road was lowered in 1839 to create a steadier slope for horse-drawn vehicles. The grand villas opposite were built on part of the Calthorpe estate in the 1840s; lower down, a few older houses near the Bloxham turn stand near the site of St John's Hospital, which flourished between the early thirteenth century and 1549.

A ROAD SIGN and tall lamp posts are the modern equivalents of the telegraph pole in the earlier view. The Banbury House Hotel has replaced or re-fronted the villas on the high pavement but the older houses lower down Oxford Road survive, and the lamp post frames the tower of St John's church.

MILTON STREET

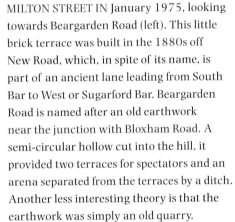

MILTON STREET IN January 1975, looking towards Beargarden Road (left). This little brick terrace was built in the 1880s off New Road, which, in spite of its name, is part of an ancient lane leading from South Bar to West or Sugarford Bar. Beargarden Road is named after an old earthwork near the junction with Bloxham Road. A semi-circular hollow cut into the hill, it provided two terraces for spectators and an arena separated from the terraces by a ditch. Another less interesting theory is that the earthwork was simply an old quarry.

A PORCH HERE and there and the odd rendered façade mark the passage of time in Milton Street, and wheelie bins have also made an appearance beside the unmade-up pathway (above). The character of the street remains intact, however, and, with the clearance of much nineteenth-century housing in central Banbury, it is now something of a rarity.

THE METHODIST CHURCH

THE WESLEYAN METHODIST church and Sunday schools in Marlborough Road, probably in the 1880s. The buildings demonstrate the size and the wealth of the Methodist community in Victorian Banbury. The church was designed by George Woodhouse and built at a cost of £6,800

between 1864 and 1865; a special fund was needed to build the spire because many Nonconformists were hostile to spires as symbols of the Established Church. The Sunday schools were added in 1882.

MARLBOROUGH ROAD METHODIST church from the junction with Marlborough Place and Albert Street (above). The church, minus a few gable end crosses, is still a powerful physical presence in central Banbury, but the Sunday schools were demolished in 1986. Marlborough Road car park filled the gap, and the tower of St Mary's church is now more prominent on the skyline.

MARLBOROUGH ROAD

LOOKING FROM MARLBOROUGH Road into High Street in April 1910 (left). Marlborough Road was laid out in 1863 on a portion of the Calthorpe Estate and one property was acquired to provide a very narrow exit to High Street; an early cautionary sign warns road users to 'Drive Slowly'.

PREMISES ALONGSIDE NO. 29 High Street were shaved off to widen the exit from Marlborough Road, and the retaining wall of Marlborough Road car park is visible to the left. The bland 1960s replacement for the White Horse pub stands on the far side of High Street but, on the right-hand corner of Marlborough Road, the side elevation of S.H. Jones & Company's old wine house maintains a strong link with the past.

THE WHEATSHEAF

A DAIMLER PURRS up a busy George Street in April 1962 (right). The Wheatsheaf pub, a stone building dating perhaps from the seventeenth century, sits a little uneasily beside the Salvation Army 'fortress' or citadel built in 1890 at a cost of £1,400. Further down, at No. 64, 'cooked meats' were on sale at the North Oxfordshire Pork & Bacon supply shop. On the left, artists' materials were being sold by Stella, a china dealer at No. 3 George Street.

THE WHEATSHEAF STILL flourishes, and the Salvation Army, which was considering a new citadel in 1978, is still based in George Street. Further down,

most old properties have gone, leaving only fading memories of Jimmy Soden the chimney sweep at No. 54 and John Butters' pawnshop, known affectionately as 'Uncle's', round the corner in Broad Street.

GEORGE STREET

ALL EYES TURN to watch a car emerge from the Red Lion tap in Fish Street, the modern George Street, in about 1910 (right). On the right, Goodway's Coach Works occupied premises on the corner of Pepper Alley; Tom Goodway recalled how they had to place vehicles on planks across the street and use a hand-operated pulley to haul them up to the first floor workshop where the man is standing. The Red Lion tap was built behind the Red Lion in 1907 and with its pebble-dashed walls and deep eaves it reflected the then fashionable Arts and Crafts movement. Further up, the four storey warehouse with hoists was used by Mawle's the ironmongers until the 1970s.

GEORGE STREET, LOOKING past Pepper Alley, can be seen in the modern photograph above.

Goodway's diversified into car painting and spraying and building repair and decorating, and the firm lasted until 1984 when Tom Goodway retired; Kalia's Indian restaurant now occupies the site. The attractive Red Lion tap was demolished in 1977 for an extension to Woolworth's, and Mawle's warehouse has also gone.

CHRIST CHURCH

CHRIST CHURCH FROM the north-west in the 1920s (right). The parish of South Banbury was created in 1846 to serve the growing population in the Cherwell Meadows; churchmen also felt that an Anglican presence was needed to counter Papal aggression and the growth of Nonconformity. Christ Church was designed by Benjamin Ferrey and built between 1851 and 1852; Samuel Wilberforce, the Bishop of Oxford, consecrated the church on 19 February 1853. Ferrey's design envisaged a tower and spire but only the tower was added in 1880.

JUBILEE COURT ON the corner of Broad Street and George Street (above). Described in 1939 as 'extremely poor and very exacting', South Banbury parish was finally merged with St Mary's in 1967 and Christ Church closed. The building was demolished in 1970 and Jubilee Court now stands on the site. To the right, the gabled Victorian house, No. 18 Broad Street, has survived this massive change.

THE COACHSMITH'S ARMS

THE OLD COACHSMITH'S Arms pub on the corner of Broad Street and Fish Street in about 1900 (below). Behind the throng of children eager to appear in the photograph, a passage led through to Church Court, which J. L. Langley recalled as having 'a most unsavoury reputation'.

Down Fish Street, the modern George Street, a sign announces premises used by C. Lampitt & Co.'s Christ Church engineering works.

BANBURY CO-OPERATIVE SOCIETY acquired the corner site and these distinctive premises, designed by A.E. Allen, were opened in August 1908. Described as 'a working man's palace in a working man's district', they provided space for the firm's grocery and tailoring departments, and featured a cash railway in both shops. The corner turret boasted the town's first electric clock. Sadly, the shop, which retains its original tiled shopfront, is currently empty.

BROAD STREET

BROAD STREET AND the Grand cinema in October 1964 (below). The first Grand cinema opened here in 1911 and Arthur Jones recalled massive queues extending round into George Street for some of the early mystery serials that were shown in weekly episodes. The new cinema, erected

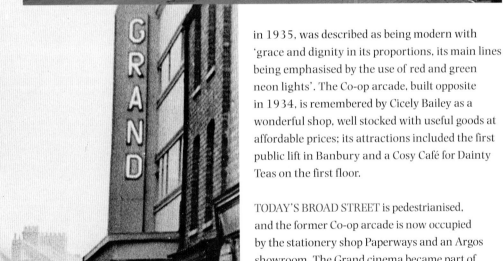

in 1935, was described as being modern with 'grace and dignity in its proportions, its main lines being emphasised by the use of red and green neon lights'. The Co-op arcade, built opposite in 1934, is remembered by Cicely Bailey as a wonderful shop, well stocked with useful goods at affordable prices; its attractions included the first public lift in Banbury and a Cosy Café for Dainty Teas on the first floor.

TODAY'S BROAD STREET is pedestrianised, and the former Co-op arcade is now occupied by the stationery shop Paperways and an Argos showroom. The Grand cinema became part of the ABC chain of cinemas in 1938 and its steel inner roof was advertised as a safety feature in case of wartime air raids. The cinema closed on 14 December 1968 and reopened as a bingo hall the following month. More recently the Chicago Rock Café until 2010, the building is now set to become The Wonderlounge.

UPPER WINDSOR STREET

UPPER WINDSOR STREET, looking north towards Windsor Terrace, August 1971 (below). The two- and three-storey brick houses, with small front gardens, were built in about 1845. The

distant Britannia pub, on the corner of Windsor Terrace, was first recorded as the Mechanics Arms in about 1869 and its later name recalled the important Britannia Works. Samuelson's Upper Works, on the site of Gardner's original foundry, lay just beyond the pub.

UPPER WINDSOR STREET is now part of the busy main road that provides a link between Oxford Road and Hennef Way. The houses are gone but the hedge fringing the car park echoes the line of their boundary fences; beyond Windsor Terrace, the Britannia has evolved into the Blarney Stone pub.

THE OLD TOWN HALL

OLD TOWN HALL Wharf in Lower Cherwell Street in February 1975 (left). The building in the background with the base of a cupola on the roof was built as Banbury's town hall in 1800. It originally stood outside the Unicorn in the Market Place and was relocated to this canal-side wharf as a warehouse in 1860 after its Victorian successor had been completed. Until recently, Chapman's of Banbury used it for storage.

THE OLD TOWN hall was restored and converted into flats as part of the adjoining Cherwell Wharf development in 2005. Paint has obliterated the bold advertisements for Palmer & Son, one of the many coal merchants that were formerly located beside the Oxford Canal, but a stone lintel on the building still announces part of the name, Old Town Hall Wharf.

CLARK'S MILL

CLARK'S MILL, OR Station Mill, from the canal bridge in Bridge Street in 1962 (opposite). Thomas Clark had the mill built in 1911 in a position that was convenient for transport by canal, railway or road. It was also powered by electricity from the power station in nearby Lower Cherwell Street. The mill supplied high grade flour to the country's leading biscuit manufacturers such as Huntley & Palmer's, Crawford's and Cadbury's. It was a noisy neighbour for local residents and covered the area with a fine dusting of white flour.

A NARROW BOAT heading for Bridge Street leads the eye towards Percy Gilkes' derelict printing works and a car park on the site of the mill. Clark's flour mill was the last of Banbury's mills to remain in production and its closure in March 1962 represented the end of an era. The impressive building was renovated and converted for the Altovar printing works in 1991 but it was largely destroyed in a spectacular fire on 16 March 1992.

Other titles published by The History Press

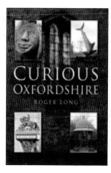

Curious Oxfordshire

ROGER LONG

Curious Oxfordshire is a fascinating guide to more than 100 sights, incidents and legends from the various parts of the county. Featuring tales of unsolved murders, witchcraft, hangings, poltergeists, underground caves and passages, 'cunning men', backswording and riots, this book is a must read for anyone with an interest in the history of Oxfordshire.

978 0 7509 4957 6

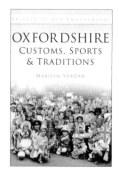

Oxfordshire Customs, Sports & Traditions

MARILYN YURDAN

The people of Oxfordshire certainly know how to enjoy themselves, and take part in many varied and remarkable customs, sports and traditions that are held annually around the county. Some of these, like the May Morning and Beating the Bounds, go back for centuries but have been altered and adapted over the years. Others include the Bampton Great Shirt race and egg jarping at Chinnor. This book features funfairs and fêtes, celebrations and carnivals, games and shows, each one a unique celebration of Oxfordshire's heritage.

978 0 7524 5743 7

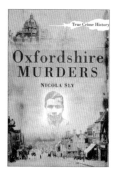

Oxfordshire Murders

NICOLA SLY

Oxfordshire Murders brings together twenty-five murderous tales, some of which were little known outside the county, and others which made national headlines. They include the deaths of two gamekeepers, brutally murdered in 1824 and 1835; Henrietta Walker, killed by her husband at Chipping Norton in 1887; and Mary Allen, shot by Harry Rowles at Cassington in the same year. Nicola Sly's carefully researched and enthralling text will appeal to anyone interested in the shady side of Oxfordshire's history.

978 0 7524 5359 0

An Oxfordshire Christmas

DAVID GREEN

This seasonal anthology of festive fare will delight Oxfordshire readers– and those further afield. Cecil Day Lewis describes 'The Christmas Tree' in verse, and Henley's first peace-time celebrations after the end of the First World War are poignantly recounted. This book also includes ghost stories, local carols and traditions and folklore, including the ancient ceremony of bringing in the boar's head at Queen's College and the Boxing Day wren hunt. *An Oxfordshire Christmas* makes an ideal gift for all who know and love the county.

978 0 7524 5313 2

Visit our website and discover thousands of other History Press books.

www.thehistorypress.co.uk